Original title:
Beneath the Snow

Copyright © 2024 Swan Charm
All rights reserved.

Author: Kätriin Kaldaru
ISBN HARDBACK: 978-9916-79-723-5
ISBN PAPERBACK: 978-9916-79-724-2
ISBN EBOOK: 978-9916-79-725-9

A Whisper from the Wintry Void

In the silence that surrounds,
Breath of frost upon the ground.
Stars like diamonds softly gleam,
Night enfolds a shivering dream.

Shadows dance in pale moonlight,
Whispers echo in the night.
Snowflakes twirl from skies above,
Nature's heart, a tale of love.

Branches bare with icy lace,
Winter's breath, a cold embrace.
Hushed and still, the world waits close,
For the dawn that nature chose.

Through the stillness, secrets flow,
In the void where soft winds blow.
A melody, sweet and rare,
Carried forth through frigid air.

As the light begins to rise,
Hope awakens with the skies.
Even in the coldest night,
Whispers promise warmth and light.

The Sighs of the Comoined White

In fields where silence lays,
The whispers softly blend,
A dance of snowflakes sways,
As twilight starts to send.

The winter's hush enfolds,
A blanket pure and bright,
Each secret gently holds,
In fading day to night.

Footprints left behind,
Trace stories lost in time,
Where dreams and hopes entwined,
In the snow's quiet rhyme.

Beneath the starry dome,
A subtle glow of peace,
In cold, yet feels like home,
As worries find release.

And so the night draws near,
With stillness as its song,
The sighs of joy and fear,
In this realm we belong.

Memories Locked in Frosted Tombs

In shadows of the past,
Where time no longer flows,
The echoes hold me fast,
As frost on memories grows.

Each breath a lingering sigh,
Embraced by icy air,
The moments whisper why,
Yet leave me unaware.

Locked deep in winter's keep,
With stories left untold,
The silence starts to creep,
In frames of white and gold.

A frozen tapestry,
Of laughter, love, and pain,
Each thread a mystery,
In frost's unyielding chain.

And still, I trace the lines,
Of joy and sorrow's dance,
In this cold world that shines,
Where memories find their chance.

Nature's Pause in the Cold Grasp

When winter's grip takes hold,
The world holds its breath tight,
In stories left untold,
As day slips into night.

The branches bare and still,
Await the springtime's call,
While time without a thrill,
Cocooned in snow will fall.

A frozen lake reflects,
The quiet of the skies,
In nature's slow aspects,
The calm before the rise.

Yet beneath the surface,
Life stirs in quiet dreams,
In patience's warm embrace,
As winter slowly gleams.

So here we stand and wait,
In wonder and in awe,
For nature, wise and late,
Will thaw what winter saw.

The Echo of Dreams in Chilled Earth

In lands of icy breath,
Where dreams begin to fade,
The quiet speaks of death,
Yet life's refrain cascades.

Within the frozen ground,
The whispers shyly bloom,
Each heartbeat softly found,
In winter's quiet room.

With every gusting breeze,
The echoes start to stir,
Recalling memories,
As thoughts begin to blur.

And in this space so stark,
Where shadows intertwine,
The dreams ignite a spark,
In the frost's pale design.

So let the echoes rise,
From chilled earth's deep embrace,
Awake the sleeping skies,
And grant the spring its grace.

In the Arms of the Cold

The wind whispers secrets, soft and low,
Blanketing the world in shimmering snow.
Trees stand silent, cloaked in white,
Under the stars, they dance in the night.

Footprints fade, lost to the frost,
Every moment cherished, never lost.
A breath of winter, crisp and clear,
In the arms of the cold, we find no fear.

Shadows grow longer, daylight turns pale,
The air carries stories, a ghostly tale.
Wrapped in warmth, we sit by the flame,
In silence we ponder, love's sweet name.

Cups of cocoa, steam rising high,
Laughter and joy, beneath the sky.
Windows frosted, patterns divine,
In the chill of the night, our hearts intertwine.

The fire flickers, shadows dance near,
Whispers of winter, faint but clear.
In the arms of the cold, we find a place,
Wrapped in comfort, an eternal embrace.

The Depths of Winter's Embrace

Snowflakes tumble, a soft ballet,
Each one unique, in the light they play.
Branches sag low, heavy with white,
The depths of winter hide day from night.

A silent forest, draped in gloom,
Whispers of frost fill every room.
The air is sharp, but hearts feel bold,
In the depths of winter, love unfolds.

Fires crackle, warmth all around,
In our embrace, solace is found.
Hot tea steaming, laughter rings clear,
In each other's arms, we shed every fear.

The world may be cold, but we're aglow,
Sunrise glimmers, a gentle show.
In this season of rest, we come alive,
In the depths of winter, we learn to thrive.

Icicles glisten, like diamonds they hang,
Nature's symphony softly sang.
In the chill of the air, we dare to dream,
In winter's embrace, all is serene.

The Hidden Stories of the Chilled Ground

Beneath the surface, secrets lie deep,
In the chilled ground, where shadows creep.
Frozen whispers of what once was here,
Tales of the past, that we hold dear.

The crunch of snow, each step reveals,
History buried beneath winter's seals.
Footprints telling of journeys embarked,
In the chilled ground, the stories are marked.

Every snowdrift, a memory's home,
In silence we gather, as frosty winds moan.
Nature's canvas, painted with care,
The hidden stories linger in the air.

As stars blanket the pitch-black night,
We share our dreams by the firelight.
In the warmth of our hearts, the past remains,
In the chilled ground, love sustains.

With every dawn, new tales arise,
As winter's beauty captivates our eyes.
In the stillness, where time appears bound,
We uncover the magic of the chilled ground.

Frosty Lullabies

The moon hangs low, a silver sphere,
Frosty lullabies, soft and near.
Singing to the night, a soothing tune,
Under the blanket of a winter moon.

The world lies still, wrapped in a sigh,
Stars wink gently, like dreams passing by.
Each flake drifts down, a tender kiss,
In frosty lullabies, we find our bliss.

Crackling embers, stories unfold,
Whispers of warmth through the bitter cold.
In this quiet moment, hearts take flight,
Frosty lullabies embrace the night.

The nightingale's song, a comfort sweet,
In the stillness, our souls meet.
Gentle caresses of winter's breath,
Whispered promises, even in death.

As dawn approaches, the dreams begin,
Frosty lullabies, beneath our skin.
We welcome the day, hearts entwined,
In the melody of winter, love defined.

Unseen Wonders of the Frigid Ground

Beneath the frost, the secrets lie,
Whispers of nature, hidden, shy.
Life blooms where the cold winds play,
A silent dance in shades of gray.

Crystal patterns lace the earth,
Each flake tells tales of winter's birth.
Footprints echo on the snow,
Marking paths where few will go.

Under the surface, roots entwine,
Drawing strength from a world divine.
Life's resilience in icy grasp,
In silence, the beauty we clasp.

Frozen streams in slumber lie,
Reflecting stars in the wintry sky.
Nature's canvas, pure and bright,
Painted in shades of ghostly white.

Look closely, see the wonders bloom,
In quiet corners, dispelling gloom.
From the cold, new life will rise,
Unseen wonders, a sweet surprise.

Memories Encased in Crystal

In the chill, time stands still,
Memories frozen, a tranquil thrill.
Each shard of ice holds a story,
Captured moments, silent glory.

The laughter echoes, crystal clear,
Captured in frost, held so dear.
A dance in snowflakes, light as air,
Whispers of joy in the frozen glare.

Through the winter, shadows dance,
Every flake a fleeting chance.
In the quiet, memories persist,
Encased in ice, we cannot resist.

Glimmers shine in the pale moonlight,
Stories spark in the deep of night.
Fragments of life, held in embrace,
Eternal moments in winter's grace.

With each breath, the past draws near,
A tapestry woven, crystal clear.
In this season, we find our place,
Memories encased in time and space.

Murmurs from the Icy Depths

Beneath the ice, a secret call,
Whispers rise from the frozen hall.
Echoes of life, so hushed and low,
Murmurs of places we long to know.

Rippling sounds through silence glide,
Hidden realms where wonders bide.
Voices trapped in the cold embrace,
Tales of the deep in a frozen space.

Crystals shimmer, light refracts,
News of the past, in frosty pacts.
Waves of memory lost in time,
Calling softly in rhythmic rhyme.

A song of winter, pure and bright,
Sings of the dark, the veiled night.
From below, the stories swell,
Murmurs of ice, a magic spell.

Listen closely, let them flow,
Feel the chill, let wonder grow.
For in these depths, a world awaits,
Murmurs from ice, opening gates.

The Depths of Frosted Stillness

In the hush of frost, a blanket spreads,
Laying softly on winter's beds.
Every breath a cloud, a sigh,
Quiet whispers, drifting sky high.

Beneath the snow, dreams gently rest,
Nature pauses, a perfect guest.
Silent thoughts in the coldest night,
Stars above twinkle, pure delight.

A tapestry woven in icy threads,
Frosted stillness where memory treads.
Every flake a story to tell,
The depths of winter, a frozen spell.

In this silence, time stands still,
Nature's heartbeat, a distant thrill.
The world asleep, wrapped tight in white,
Harmony found in the depths of night.

In this stillness, we find our peace,
A quiet moment that will not cease.
For in frost's embrace, dreams come alive,
The depths of stillness, where spirits thrive.

Thoughts Wrapped in Frost

Morning whispers in the air,
Thoughts wrapped in frost everywhere.
Nature's quilt of silver sheen,
Hides the dreams of what has been.

Branches lace the sky so bright,
Casting shadows in the light.
A breath of winter, soft and clear,
Echoes gently, sweet yet near.

Silent paths that weave and wind,
Stories of the past, entwined.
Each crystal flake a tale unfolds,
In the warmth of hearts it holds.

In the stillness, time stands still,
Moments captured, memories spill.
Every glance, a fleeting thought,
In this serenity, peace is sought.

As the sun dips low and fades,
Shadows dance in twilight glades.
A final sigh, the day departs,
With the frost, it warms our hearts.

The Essence of Life Under Winter's Canopy

Beneath a canopy of gray,
Life stirs softly, in its way.
Gentle whispers, secret dreams,
Flow like rivers, quiet streams.

Icicles hang like fragile glass,
Reflecting moments as they pass.
In stillness, hope begins to grow,
Beneath the layers of soft snow.

Birds weave songs of distant lands,
While nature guards with tender hands.
In the silence, energy brews,
Color waiting for its cues.

Amidst the cold, a warmth remains,
In every drop, in every vein.
Buds are resting, dreams to show,
With the spring, they will all glow.

Winter's breath, a gentle sigh,
Promising life as days go by.
Underneath the frost's embrace,
Awaits the world, a lively space.

Embrace of the Silent Ground

Under blankets of pure white,
A soft embrace, a tranquil night.
Hidden lives in quiet verse,
Nature's lullaby, soft and terse.

Roots reach down, in silence grow,
Resilient strength, beneath the snow.
Connected deep, in sacred ground,
Life's foundation, subtly found.

Whispers of the earth's own heart,
In every pulse, a vital part.
Holding secrets, dreams are sown,
In silent cradles, love is grown.

As the moon casts shadows long,
In stillness, we hear nature's song.
In the dark, life finds a way,
To rise anew with break of day.

Embrace the quiet, just a pause,
For in stillness lies the cause.
A promise held in earth's embrace,
Awaits the sun, to warm this space.

Echoes of Flora in Frozen Silence

Amidst the quiet, flowers sleep,
In frozen silence, secrets keep.
Their colors muted, dreams on hold,
Yet echoes of their tales unfold.

Petals curled in winter's grasp,
Awaiting spring's gentle clasp.
In icy stillness, life remains,
Whispered truths in cold terrains.

Every bud a sigh of hope,
In nature's weave, a fragile rope.
Beneath the frost, a whisper grows,
Of vibrant blooms the world still knows.

With every breeze, a story shared,
Of summer's warmth, now long prepared.
In the chill, there's beauty found,
As echoes dance from frozen ground.

When winter wanes and melts away,
Flora's laughter fills the day.
In frozen silence, life shall thrive,
As echoes blossom, come alive.

Beneath Winter's Heavy Quilt

Snowflakes dance through the air,
They blanket the world below.
Each branch draped in white,
In silence, the whispers grow.

Chill winds croon a soft song,
Nature rests in hibernation.
Footprints are quickly erased,
In this tranquil isolation.

The moon casts a silver sheen,
Across the frostbitten ground.
Stars twinkle like distant dreams,
In the stillness, peace is found.

Beneath winter's heavy quilt,
Life waits for the warm sun's kiss.
Hope is alive, though unseen,
In the heart's quiet abyss.

Each breath of winter's air,
Fills the soul with calm delight.
In the clutch of frosty nights,
The world sleeps, wrapped in white.

A World Hiding in Crystal Stillness

Icicles hang like jewels bright,
Glistening in the pale moonlight.
The air is crisp, the world is clear,
In quietude, all is near.

A frozen river flows so slow,
Reflecting dreams, a soft glow.
Beneath the ice, life stirs awake,
A secret world, still and opaque.

The branches bow beneath their weight,
Nature's art, a regal state.
Each breath visible in the cold,
A story whispered, softly told.

Snowflakes kiss the earth's warm skin,
In this stillness, life begins.
Wonders hidden, softly breathe,
In the quiet, hearts believe.

A world of beauty wrapped in frost,
In the calm, nothing is lost.
Amidst the quiet, dreams take flight,
In crystal stillness, pure delight.

The Secret Life of the Sleeping Earth

Buried deep beneath the snow,
The earth sleeps, silent and low.
Roots entwined in a gentle embrace,
Awaiting spring's warm, soft grace.

Seeds lie dormant, hidden away,
Living dreams in cold delay.
In the dark, life holds its breath,
Cradled close, awaiting death.

Whispers echo in the night,
From soil rich and mammals slight.
Creatures stir in secret ways,
In winter's depth, the heart still plays.

The sun will rise, the thaw will come,
As life awakens, beating drum.
Underneath this frozen crust,
Lies the promise, pure and just.

From slumber's hold, the earth will rise,
With vibrant blooms 'neath sunny skies.
The secret life shall soon unfold,
In colors bright and stories told.

Murmurs from the Snow-Cloaked Abyss

In the depths of winter's grip,
Soft murmurs rise and gently slip.
Shadows dance in the cold, pale light,
Secrets whispered through the night.

Beneath layers of pristine snow,
Life pulses softly, ebb and flow.
A heartbeat felt within the frost,
In stillness, nothing is lost.

The wind carries tales untold,
Of journeys warm, and hearts bold.
In the abyss, shadows play,
Waiting for the break of day.

Crystals shimmer, refracting hope,
In the void, there's a wider scope.
Cloaked in white, the world holds tight,
To dreams that linger in the night.

When spring arrives to melt this chill,
The whispers change, begin to thrill.
From the abyss, life will ascend,
In winter's depth, there's always an end.

Beneath the Icy Surface

Underneath the frozen lake,
A secret world lies still,
Where fish dart through icy veins,
And silence bends to will.

Crystals glisten in the dark,
Like stars that drift below,
Whispers haunt the frigid air,
Of stories left untold.

Frosted roots grip ancient stones,
As time slips softly by,
Each layer holds a memory,
Beneath the winter sky.

A pulse beneath the icy shell,
Life waits for spring's embrace,
To break the stillness, thaw the heart,
And bring forgotten grace.

So we tread with gentle steps,
Above this hidden sphere,
Hoping for the warmth to come,
And banish all our fear.

The Cradle of Winter's Sleep

Snowflakes dance on silent nights,
In blankets white they lay,
Nature sighs and slips away,
To cradle dreams of May.

Trees stand guard with arms outstretched,
A promise held in frost,
Whispers weave through branches bare,
Of all that's gained or lost.

Beneath the layers of soft quilt,
Life waits without a peep,
In shadows deep and quiet nooks,
The world is hushed in sleep.

A lullaby of frozen air,
Cradles each frozen breath,
In winter's hold, we find our peace,
Embracing life and death.

So let us find our slumber here,
In this majestic pause,
For every night must yield to light,
And time shall take its cause.

The Winter Garden's Secrets

In winter's hush, the garden sleeps,
Beneath a cloak of snow,
Hidden wonders lie in wait,
For spring to come and show.

Frosted petals, colors fade,
Yet beauty lingers still,
In every branch and leaf turned brown,
A promise to fulfill.

The whispers of the winter breeze,
Tell tales of growing things,
Of roots that anchor deep below,
And hope that softly sings.

Each seed rests in a cozy womb,
Awaiting time to bloom,
A secret world beneath the snow,
With life that's not yet doomed.

So let us wander quietly,
Through gardens cloaked in ice,
For nature holds her secrets close,
And dreams will soon suffice.

Illumination in a Frozen World

The moonlight casts a silver hue,
On fields of sparkling frost,
A canvas vast, untouched by time,
Where warmth and light are lost.

Each flake a jewel, unique and grand,
As shadows dance and play,
In this frozen world of stark contrast,
That glimmers night and day.

The silence sings a haunting song,
Of beauty in the cold,
Each breath a mist, each heartbeat strong,
In twilight's grasp we hold.

Stars reflect on icy ponds,
Creating worlds anew,
A tapestry of dreams and hopes,
In every shade and hue.

So let us walk this crystal path,
With wonder in our hearts,
For life can shine in frozen realms,
Where light and shadow part.

Warmth Within the Winter's Grip

In the quiet dusk, the snowflakes fall,
Whispering secrets, soft and small.
The fire crackles, a gentle glow,
Wraps us in warmth from the bitter snow.

Cups of cocoa and laughter abound,
As frost weaves patterns, all around.
A blanket of peace, a tender quilt,
With love and comfort, our hearts are filled.

The chill outside, it bites and stings,
Yet inside us, a soft warmth clings.
Together we create our own bright light,
Against the cold, we'll hold on tight.

Nature's beauty, stark but fair,
Glistening branches, beyond compare.
Every breath a cloud, in the icy air,
But in our hearts, the flame is rare.

So let the winter take its hold,
In our embrace, we'll never grow cold.
The warmth within is love's sweet song,
Together, we know, this is where we belong.

Shadows of the Winter's Kiss

Silent whispers in the frigid night,
Stars above shine, ever so bright.
The moon casts shadows on the frozen ground,
As winter's breath moves softly around.

Branches bare, silhouettes dance,
Under the glow, as if in a trance.
In the chill, there's a haunting grace,
Nature's beauty, a stark embrace.

Footsteps crunch on the snowy trail,
As night descends, the spirits prevail.
Hushed tones of nature share their tale,
In the shadows, whispers never pale.

Amidst the frost, an echoing song,
In every heartbeat, where we belong.
Winter's kiss, both cold and fair,
Leaves behind traces; still, we care.

So let the shadows guide our way,
Through the darkness, come what may.
Each breath a mist, in the moonlit churn,
In winter's heart, for warmth, we yearn.

Together, we walk this night so still,
Embracing the chill with unwavering will.
Through the shadows of winter's gentle call,
With open hearts, we'll never fall.

Dormant Spirits of the Chill

Beneath the snow, the earth does sleep,
In silent slumber, its secrets keep.
Dormant spirits, wrapped in dreams,
Awaiting spring's warm, gentle beams.

Frozen whispers echo softly here,
In the hushed silence, we draw near.
Nature's lullaby, sweet and low,
In the heart of winter, we feel it grow.

Branches cradle the weight of frost,
Yet in their stillness, nothing is lost.
Life's cycles turn, though it seems so bare,
There's beauty in waiting, in the frigid air.

The world is hushed; a moment divine,
As we pause to reflect on the design.
Each flake that falls adds to the lore,
Of dreams buried deep, on winter's floor.

In this stillness, we find our peace,
As restless hearts long for release.
Spring will come, with colors so bright,
But for now, we live in the quiet night.

Beneath the Frost's Embrace

Under the blanket of winter's sway,
Nature rests in a serene display.
Frosted windows, a delicate lace,
In this stillness, we find our place.

Icicles hang like jeweled tears,
Reflecting back our hopes and fears.
Each breath we take, a cloud in the air,
In the chill, we dance with care.

Bare trees stand, like guardians old,
Holding stories yet to be told.
Within their hearts, the promise waits,
Of vibrant blooms and lighter fates.

So let us walk through winter's grace,
Finding joy in this sacred space.
Beneath the frost, life's pulse resides,
In whispered dreams, the magic hides.

As snowflakes twirl and gently fall,
We embrace the quiet, the beauty of all.
In winter's sleep, hope starts to gleam,
For warmth returns, a cherished dream.

Echoes from the Subterranean Chill

In the depths where shadows dwell,
Faint whispers rise from the ground.
Ghostly echoes softly swell,
Carrying tales of silence profound.

Frozen roots embrace the cold,
Memories buried, deep and still.
Secret stories waiting, bold,
In the heart of winter's thrill.

Where darkness wraps its quiet shroud,
And frost entangles ancient stone,
A spectral hymn hums aloud,
In the chill, we are not alone.

Beneath the snow, our fears lie bare,
Silent truths that time forgot.
In shadows, we lay our prayer,
For peace found in the icy knot.

So listen close, in every sigh,
The breath of ages fills the air.
In the dark, we cannot die,
For echoes linger everywhere.

Silent Histories in Ice

Frosted pages turn with grace,
Chronicles of a frozen past.
Each crystal fleck a hidden space,
Where stories linger, shadows cast.

Glaciers hold our whispered dreams,
In their grip, we fade away.
Silent histories in icy beams,
Guarding secrets of yesterday.

Footprints lost beneath the tread,
Of those who've walked, now mere smoke.
Every layer, a tale unsaid,
In winter's grasp, we are bespoke.

Freezing winds carry the names,
Of forgotten souls in the night.
In the stillness, a spark remains,
Each flake a ghost, a breath of light.

So wrap yourself in this embrace,
Where frosted memories unite.
In silence, we find our place,
In histories that are alight.

Memories Locked in Winter's Grasp

Under the mantle of serene white,
Lies a treasure trove of the lost.
Each snowflake dances in soft light,
Holding memories, never tossed.

Buried deep in sleep's embrace,
Echoes flicker, a sigh, a plea.
Frozen dreams in this quiet space,
Whispers of what is yet to be.

Branches sway with a gentle hush,
Snowflakes falling, soft like lace.
In the quiet, hear the rush,
Of past and future's warm embrace.

Captured time in the frost's hold,
Each moment, a memory framed.
With every breath, stories unfold,
In winter's grasp, nothing's shamed.

So raise a glass to icy fates,
As we dance with what once was fair.
In the chill, our heart resonates,
For all that lingers in the air.

The Depths of the Icy Expanse

Beneath the waves of freezing blue,
Lies a world both vast and dark.
Where secrets dwell, and hopes renew,
In silence, reigns an icy spark.

Caverns echo with ancient cries,
In the depths, all is still and slow.
Where the heart of winter lies,
Time stands still, yet does not go.

In the chill, dreams intertwine,
As shadows play across the floor.
In the darkness, moments shine,
Reflecting what we can explore.

Icebergs float like thoughts unseen,
In their edges, a story waits.
Within their grace, all has been,
Forever sealed, like ancient gates.

So dive into the icy night,
Unravel yarns of lost delight.
In the depths, discover might,
For there, in silence, hearts take flight.

Whispers of Winter's Veil

Silent flakes drift down, soft and light,
Blanketing the world in pure white.
Barren branches softly sway,
Nature holds its breath, at play.

Chill winds carry secrets untold,
Stories of warmth in the bitter cold.
A hushed symphony fills the air,
Winter whispers with gentle care.

Pines stand tall, adorned in frost,
In this stillness, nothing is lost.
Night descends with a starry cloak,
In dreams of warmth, our hearts invoke.

Footprints trace in the glimmering snow,
Each step whispers where we go.
In the quiet, magic begins,
As winter's mystery gently spins.

Hope lies hidden beneath the ice,
Nature's canvas, a peaceful slice.
As time flows on, seasons will shift,
In winter's grip, we find our gift.

Secrets of the Frozen Earth

Beneath the frost, a story lies,
A world concealed 'neath the winter skies.
Roots intertwine in slumber deep,
Guarding secrets that winter keeps.

Whispers of growth wrapped in snow's embrace,
Silent cycles, a gentle pace.
Each frozen breath a tale of grace,
Nature pauses, a timeless space.

Crystals shimmer, like stars from above,
Nurturing dreams with warmth and love.
In the hush, the earth reclaims,
Setting the stage for spring's new games.

The air is crisp, yet life still thrives,
In hidden realms, where beauty strives.
Under the ice, patience holds sway,
As winter's night yields to day.

Nature sleeps but never is gone,
Awakening soon to the light of dawn.
Each frost-kissed morn, a promise made,
In frozen silence, life won't fade.

Echoes Under the Ice

Echoes ripple through the silent deep,
Beneath the surface, secrets creep.
Frozen whispers of a vibrant past,
In icy chambers, memories cast.

Shadows linger in the twilight glow,
Veiled within the winter's flow.
In the stillness, life holds its breath,
As time dances with dreams of death.

Each fleeting moment, a tale retold,
In the realm of the brave and bold.
Resilience battles against the chill,
In the frozen depths, time stands still.

Gypsy winds waltz with snowflakes light,
Eclipsing shadows, making them bright.
With every sparkle, a thousand songs,
In the heart of winter, where beauty belongs.

Through ice and silence, hope cannot die,
Tethered to whispers that gently sigh.
In the cosmos of frost, life finds a way,
In echoes of winter, we dare to stay.

Hidden Life in White Hush

In the stillness, life takes its form,
Beneath the snow, it keeps warm.
Tiny creatures in secret play,
In winter's cradle, they dream away.

Soft shadows scurry beneath the frost,
Murmurs of life, never lost.
Hidden whispers of emerald green,
Awaiting spring, a dance unseen.

The blanket of white tells no lie,
As some hearts beat under the sky.
Frosted leaves hide, still and meek,
In the hush, nature's pulse we seek.

The world lies quiet, a treasure chest,
Holding secrets, it keeps at rest.
Life lingers on, in the cold embrace,
Waiting for warmth, to bring its grace.

In the whiteness, thrum of a beat,
Nature's heartbeat, steady and fleet.
Hidden life stirs under slumber's song,
And from the hush, spring will belong.

Echoes of Frosted Dreams

In the hush of winter's breath,
Whispers dance on frozen streams.
Stars above a twilight sketch,
Lost in echoes of our dreams.

Snowflakes twirl like fleeting thoughts,
Softly landing, time stands still.
Frosted night, a world forgot,
Blankets silence, softly chill.

Crystals gleam on branches bare,
Moonlight weaves through icy breath.
In this heart, a tender care,
Amidst the beauty lies our depth.

Darkness wraps the earth in peace,
Nights adorned in silver lace.
With each sigh, our worries cease,
In winter's calm, we find our place.

Hidden Life in frost's Embrace

Beneath the cover of white snow,
Life waits patiently to bloom.
Roots entwined where cold winds blow,
Hidden dreams in winter's tomb.

Silent whispers of the woods,
Animals in slumber deep.
Nature's pause, a solitude,
In frost's embrace, secrets keep.

Thorns and brambles wrapped in frost,
Hold the tales of seasons past.
In the stillness, nothing lost,
Life prepares, this chill won't last.

Time draws close with every night,
Sunrise soon will break the spell.
Beneath the frost, a heart beats bright,
Waiting for spring's sweet farewell.

The Silence of the Winter Hearth

Crackling wood fills up the room,
Whispers soft in shadows cast.
Warmth dissolves the winter's gloom,
In this hearth, the world is vast.

Stories told around the flame,
Moments shared, a priceless gift.
Each one holds a cherished name,
In the silence, spirits lift.

Outside, snowflakes continue to fall,
Filling up the night with white.
But here, there's a warmth for all,
In the glow, our hearts ignite.

Where memories and dreams collide,
Time slows down, a sacred space.
In the hearth, we choose to bide,
Finding solace in this place.

Veiled in White

A quiet world in layers dressed,
Whispers float on chilly air.
Every tree, in snow, confessed,
Nature hides without a care.

Patterns woven, crisp and bright,
Footsteps lost in winter's song.
Veil of white, a pure delight,
Here in silence, we belong.

Branches bow with heavy crowns,
Burdened by the gentle snows.
Stillness wraps the sleepy towns,
In this peace, our spirit grows.

Evening settles, stars appear,
Glistening on a tranquil night.
Veiled in white, we hold so dear,
Dreams arise beneath their light.

Murmurs of the Shivering Ground

Beneath the frost, whispers breathe,
Secrets held in winter's sheath.
Silent tales in chilly night,
Echoed dreams in pale moonlight.

Shadows dance on frozen ground,
Nature's pulse, a subtle sound.
Every flake, a story told,
In the silence, life unfolds.

Roots entwine, a hidden thread,
Cradling memories long since dead.
The earth shivers, soft and deep,
In the dark, it starts to weep.

Winds carry a haunting song,
Where the lost and cold belong.
In the hush, the echoes play,
Murmurs of a faded day.

Yet, within this frozen peace,
Life prepares for warm release.
Beauty lingers, held in time,
Nature's notes in whispered rhyme.

The Quiet Below

Beneath the crust, a stillness lies,
In the depths, where silence sighs.
Layers thick with ancient lore,
Resting dreams and stories sore.

Roots stretch wide beneath the chill,
Absorbing whispers, quiet thrill.
In the dark, the heartbeats sound,
Nature's pulse in earth unbound.

The frost caresses ancient stone,
Each silent moment feels like home.
Echoes of a life once free,
Trapped below, in reverie.

Hidden gems in shadows cling,
The warmth of spring starts to sing.
Underneath, a world awaits,
Guarded by the frozen gates.

Soon the thaw will break the ice,
Bringing forth a sweet device.
Awakening from slumbered show,
Life emerges from the quiet below.

Frosted Secrets of the Slumbering Soil

Secrets wrapped in snowy white,
Beneath the stars that twinkle bright.
In the soil, the stories lay,
Frosted dreams come out to play.

Time stands still in frozen air,
Whispers linger everywhere.
Nature holds its breath in awe,
Silent guardians of the law.

Underneath the icy sheet,
Life is resting, calm and neat.
Silent promise, life will bloom,
Breaking free from winter's gloom.

Shadows weave through night's embrace,
Frosted secrets find their place.
Nature's blanket, soft and cold,
Cradles treasures, yet untold.

As the warmth begins to creep,
Awakening from secret sleep.
Frosted whispers rise and soar,
Revealing tales forevermore.

Dreaming in the Icy Stillness

In the hush of winter's breath,
Dreams are woven, life from death.
Icy stillness wraps around,
Holding hopes beneath the ground.

Moonlight casts a silver hue,
Painting landscapes crisp and new.
In the cold, a heartbeat goes,
Nature's rhythm, softly flows.

Winds serenade with gentle tones,
Carrying stories, ancient groans.
Each flake, a thought that drifts away,
In the stillness, dreams at play.

Crystals sparkle in the night,
Reflecting visions, pure and bright.
Within the frost, the world stands still,
In this moment, all is will.

Soon the thaw will start to break,
Shaking loose from winter's ache.
Yet in this time, we feel the call,
Dreaming in the icy thrall.

Secrets Lurking in Winter's Mask

Beneath the snow, the shadows creep,
Silent stories, secrets deep.
Whispers carried on the breeze,
Frozen hearts, lost memories.

Branches bare, their tales untold,
Wrap around the dark and cold.
Footprints vanish, dreams collide,
In this hush, the truth can hide.

Moonlit nights, a silver glow,
Casting light on all we know.
Secrets linger, frost to thaw,
In winter's grasp, we find the awe.

Barely heard, a gentle sigh,
Echoes of the days gone by.
With each flake, stories fall,
Winter speaks, its voice to all.

In the quiet, a world awaits,
Nature dances, and patiently waits.
Behind the veil, a spark remains,
In every crystal, life sustains.

Whispers of Winter's Veil

Softly falling, shadows blend,
Winter whispers, night to lend.
In the hush, we pause and breathe,
Nature's art, a breath to weave.

Glistening branches, cloaked in white,
Sparkling dreams in frosty light.
Frozen rivers tell no lies,
Reflecting stars in winter skies.

Brittle leaves, a crunch beneath,
Secrets hidden, nature's sheath.
A tapestry of cold and warmth,
Life preserved, a quiet charm.

Through the veil, the sun will shine,
Melting truths in soft design.
Once again, life will emerge,
From winter's cloak, a vibrant surge.

In the silence, hearts awake,
Beneath the weight of snowflakes quake.
Whispers linger in the air,
Carrying hope, a gentle prayer.

Secrets of the Frozen Earth

Underneath the icy glide,
Earth's embrace, where secrets bide.
Silent whispers, deep and low,
Guardians of the frost and snow.

Crumbling bark, a story told,
Nature's heart, both fierce and bold.
Roots entwined in winter's grasp,
Hold the past within their clasp.

Crystals formed in winter's chill,
Glisten soft, like nature's will.
Echoes of the ice age's scream,
Frozen fragments of a dream.

Life awaits in slumber deep,
Nature stirs; she does not sleep.
Seeds of promise buried tight,
Waiting for the spring's first light.

Unlocking frozen, buried lore,
The earth awakens to explore.
In the thaw, the world will rise,
Revealing secrets, vast and wise.

Under the Crystal Blanket

Where frost lays down a diamond sheet,
The world transforms, a silent feat.
Underneath this crystal dome,
The earth reclaims its frozen home.

Fields of white, a soft embrace,
Nature dons a purest face.
In the depths, where warmth remains,
Promise lingers, joy sustains.

Each flake tells a tale of old,
Whispers of warmth, dreams unfold.
Rustling winds, a soft caress,
Winter's touch, a sweet finesse.

Underneath, the heartbeats thrum,
Life persists, though cold may come.
A peaceful hush, a tranquil balm,
In this stillness, winter's calm.

As seasons turn, the blanket shifts,
Revealing life that winter gifts.
Beneath the frost, a pulse is found,
Under this blanket, love's profound.

The Silence of Snowbound Secrets

Whispers drift on frosty air,
In snowfall's hush, a cloaked affair.
The world beneath a shimmering shroud,
Secrets kept, in silence proud.

Branches bow with burdened grace,
Nature's stillness, a sacred place.
Footprints vanish, tales untold,
In winter's grasp, memories unfold.

Crystals sparkle like hidden dreams,
Silent echoes, soft moonbeams.
Each flake a story yet to share,
In this frozen realm, none compare.

Shadows dance in twilight's glow,
Veils of white conceal below.
In the calm, a heartbeat thuds,
Winter's breath, wrapped in buds.

As dawn breaks, the world awakes,
The spell of winter gently shakes.
The secrets kept, now softly known,
In snowbound silence, seeds have grown.

Winter's Lullaby for the Buried Field

Softly falls the blanket white,
A cradle woven, pure delight.
Fields, now hushed beneath the snow,
Dreaming deep, where roots will grow.

Blankets cover life anew,
Nature's sleep, a tranquil view.
Whispers float on frosty breeze,
Winter's song brings gentle ease.

Stars peek through the starlit night,
Guiding dreams with tender light.
Crickets hush, the owls awake,
In the quiet, rhythms quake.

Snowflakes twirl in midnight's gaze,
An icy dance, a breathless phase.
The buried field, a heart concealed,
In winter's lullaby, gently healed.

Time stands still in silver beams,
Nature's hush, a world that dreams.
When spring arrives, life will burst,
But for now, a frost's embrace, our thirst.

Hidden Rhythms of Frozen Life

Beneath the ice, a heartbeat stirs,
In stillness, life quietly purrs.
Roots entwined in silent cheer,
Whispers echo, soft yet clear.

Frosty breaths weave secret tunes,
Melodies beneath the dunes.
Nature's pulse, a soft refrain,
In frozen depths, a primal gain.

Bubbles rise in chilly streams,
Frozen currents hold their dreams.
Underneath, the rhythms sway,
A symphony of night and day.

Life in slumber, shadows dance,
In winter's grip, a hidden chance.
Silent whispers, life persists,
In the chill, the warmth exists.

Awake with spring, the world will leap,
But for now, the secrets keep.
Frozen whispers, hidden and bold,
In every story yet untold.

The Soft Pulse of Winter's Heartbeat

A tranquil hush envelops night,
Winter's breath, soft and light.
Branches sway in icy grace,
Nature's calm, a warm embrace.

Underneath the snowy crest,
Life lays low, in quiet rest.
Crystals glint like dreams concealed,
In every flake, a truth revealed.

The moonlight spills on frozen ground,
Awakening the silent sound.
Resting hearts in rhythmic beat,
Winter's song, both soft and sweet.

Echoes of a softened cry,
In winter's chill, the spirits fly.
Frozen pulses, life in trance,
In the stillness, take your chance.

Soon the thaw will break the spell,
But for now, all is well.
The pulse of winter, strong and true,
Echoes softly, just for you.

Flickers of Life in Winter's Hold

In shadows deep, the embers glow,
Whispers of warmth in the crisp, cold snow.
A flicker here, a spark of light,
Hopes held close in the winter night.

Silent dreams in a frozen stream,
Nature's breath in a silver gleam.
Through the frost, each heartbeat flows,
Life persists where the chill wind blows.

Branches bare, yet they can dream,
Of vibrant blooms in a sunlit beam.
Beneath the ice, the roots grow strong,
A symphony played, though the world feels wrong.

Stars peek down from their velvet shroud,
Softly watching, ever proud.
In the darkness, a promise made,
Of spring to come—the winter's fade.

Small gifts of life, like a flicker's dance,
Braving the cold with a daring glance.
In every frost, a story told,
Of warmth and hope, in winter's hold.

Beneath the Chill of a Graying Sky

Under heavy clouds, a silence falls,
The hush of winter softly calls.
Each breath a mist, as shadows creep,
Secrets whispered where the pine trees sleep.

Frosted whispers in the biting air,
Echoing dreams that linger there.
Beneath the chill, the earth holds tight,
Awaiting warmth, the end of night.

Gray branches sway, a gentle sigh,
As time drifts slowly, like a lullaby.
The world in stillness, wrapped in gray,
Yearns for color that will find its way.

From frozen ground, a pulse remains,
The promise of life in dormant veins.
Beneath the chill, hope's ember glows,
Waiting for spring to break its prose.

A tapestry of white and gray,
Nature paints in its own way.
Beneath the chill, life starts to wake,
Embracing warmth for the springtime's sake.

Quiet Spirits of the Frost-Kissed Earth

In the quietude, the spirits roam,
Wandering whispers find their home.
Through crackling leaves, the stories glide,
Of chilly nights where shadows bide.

Frost-kissed earth, a silver sheet,
Hiding secrets from weary feet.
The breath of winter on every stone,
Carrying tales of all alone.

Softly calling with a gentle breeze,
Echoes of warmth from ancient trees.
Silent guardians of the night,
In frozen realms they hold their light.

Hushed are the voices, yet alive,
In this stillness, spirits thrive.
Though the world sleeps, dreams take flight,
Under the glow of a pale moonlight.

Frost-kissed earth, with layers fierce,
Weaving magic, where hearts pierce.
In their embrace, quiet souls beckon,
To cherish the frost, their whispers reckon.

The Hidden Garden of Snowflakes

In the twilight's hush, a garden sleeps,
Where snowflakes dance, and magic leaps.
Each flake a gem, a tale unspun,
Whirling softly till the day is done.

Beneath the cover, the world is still,
A crisp white blanket, a wondrous thrill.
Here lie dreams in a frosty bed,
Awaiting the sun, where they'll be led.

Branches wear coats of glistening white,
The hidden garden, a pure delight.
In silence deep, the secrets bloom,
Whispers of life in winter's gloom.

Crystals form in the evening's glow,
Creating realms where silence flows.
Amidst the cold, hope begins to sprout,
In this hidden garden, without a doubt.

When springtime stirs, its breath comes near,
The hidden garden will reappear.
But till that time, let the snowflakes play,
In a winter's night, they'll find their way.

Twilight Tales of the Frozen Realm

In twilight's glow, the shadows play,
Whispers of frost, where night meets day.
Under a blanket of shimmering white,
Stories unfurl in the quiet night.

Crystals twinkle with secrets old,
The breath of winter, a tale retold.
Nature's canvas, a masterpiece spun,
Beneath the watchful gaze of the sun.

In silence deep, the stars take flight,
Chasing the dreams that linger in sight.
Each flake a promise, a wish to keep,
In the frozen realm where shadows seep.

Bears in slumber, tucked in their dens,
While winds hum softly, like ancient friends.
Echoes of joy in the crisp night air,
Of twilight tales that beckon to share.

A lantern glows where the hearth burns bright,
Stirring the heart with its warming light.
Within these tales, the magic unwinds,
In the frozen realm, where love still binds.

Secrets of the Snow-Covered World

Secrets are whispered in the snow,
Where silent footsteps softly go.
Under a veil of shimmering light,
Nature's wonders come into sight.

Frosty branches stretch towards the sky,
While the distant echoes of laughter fly.
Winter's embrace, a gentle caress,
Holding the world in a shimmering dress.

Each glistening flake a story to tell,
Of frozen oceans, where silence fell.
Among the pines, the shadows weave,
In this world of white, we dare to believe.

Winter's breath is a sigh so sweet,
A chill that makes the heart skip a beat.
In the snow-covered world, secrets unfold,
In whispers of warmth, and dreams of gold.

As twilight descends with a blanket serene,
The night wears dreams like a silken sheen.
In this realm where the cold winds swirl,
We find the magic of the snow-covered world.

Murmuring Dreams Underneath

Murmurs of dreams beneath the frost,
In silent echoes, we count the cost.
Hidden desires in the moonlight's glow,
Embrace the stillness, let worries go.

Under layers of white, stories sleep,
Waiting for spring when their roots will leap.
Frozen wishes drift through the air,
Whispering secrets, sweet and rare.

In icy breaths, the world seems to sigh,
While stars shimmer softly in the sky.
Winter's touch is a gentle hand,
Caressing the dreams that we had planned.

Among the shadows, the dreams are spun,
In the quiet night, we find our fun.
Each breath of snow brings a promise true,
That spring will follow, and life renew.

Murmuring dreams, like songs on the breeze,
Dance with the night, with effortless ease.
For beneath the frost, where silence reigns,
There lies the promise of brighter gains.

Drawing Breath in the Cold

Drawing breath in the chill of night,
With every puff, a cloud takes flight.
Nature's whisper in frostbitten air,
Inviting us to linger and dare.

In blankets of snow, the world is still,
A canvas for dreams, a soft-spoken thrill.
The stars above twinkle like dreams,
In this frozen world, nothing is as it seems.

When winter's breath wraps us tight,
And shadows dance in pale moonlight.
We find our warmth in stories shared,
In the flicker of fires, our hearts are bared.

With every heartbeat, the cold ignites,
A passion for life, that never fights.
In the hush of night, we come alive,
Drawing breath that helps us thrive.

For within the chill, there lies a fire,
A spark of warmth, a deep desire.
In the cold, we find what makes us whole,
Drawing breath, breathing in the soul.

The Land of Forgotten Echoes

In shadows long and whispers low,
A place where distant voices flow.
Among the hills, the silence claims,
Forgotten dreams, and broken names.

Ghostly footprints in the sand,
Memories clutched by time's cold hand.
Every sigh, a tale retold,
In ancient tones, both meek and bold.

Time stands still, yet moves ahead,
In this land where echoes tread.
In hazy mist, the stories blend,
As heartbeats mark the journey's end.

Once vibrant voices fade away,
Like leaves that flutter, fall, and sway.
Yet still they call, a tender plea,
In forgotten lands, we find the key.

So listen close to windswept sighs,
In the heart where the silence lies.
Embrace the murmurs, deep and wise,
In the land where our sorrow flies.

Beneath the Blanket of Time

With layers deep, the earth does sleep,
Beneath the frost, in dreams we keep.
Each moment wrapped in gentle care,
Lost in thoughts, the world laid bare.

Winter whispers secrets slow,
In the heart where memories grow.
Stillness reigns, no steps to trace,
A silent dance, a tender grace.

The stars above, like diamonds gleam,
In the dark, they weave a dream.
A tapestry of hope and light,
Guiding souls through velvet night.

Time sways softly, a lullaby,
In the hush where shadows lie.
Beneath the stars, the earth draws close,
To cradle those we cherish most.

As dawn creeps in, the world awakes,
It sheds the skin of frost that aches.
Beneath the blanket, life will rise,
In radiance beneath the skies.

The Quietude of the Winter Earth

In stillness wrapped, the winter's breath,
A sacred hush, a pause from death.
The world adorned in icy lace,
Embraces all with a soft grace.

The air is crisp, a gentle bite,
While shadows stretch, embracing night.
A quiet peace falls on the ground,
In silent rhythms, solace found.

Trees stand tall, their limbs embraced,
By layers white, the past displaced.
A solemn promise in the chill,
That warmth will come; the heart shall fill.

Snowflakes drift, in whispered prayer,
Each one unique, beyond compare.
A tapestry, both pure and true,
A world renewed, and born anew.

In quietude, the earth reflects,
The beauty found in small respects.
Though winter reigns, the cycle flows,
In every heart, the warmth still grows.

Life's Promise in the Frigid Shadows

In shadows cast by winter's might,
Life's promise glows, a tender light.
Amidst the chill, the heartbeats thrum,
Resilient whispers, we shall come.

Through frosted fields, the dreams abide,
While frigid paths we bravely stride.
A flicker of hope, a secret told,
In hues of silver, bright and bold.

Footsteps trace through frozen streams,
In every crack, a tale of dreams.
Though darkness falls, the spirit sings,
In every heart, new life takes wing.

From bitter cold, the warmth survives,
With every breath, the promise thrives.
In winter's grasp, we stand as one,
Awake and waiting for the sun.

Life's gentle pulse beneath the snow,
Promises made in stillness grow.
In frigid shadows, hope remains,
For every heart that dares to reign.

Echoes of Warmth Under Chilled Layers

Beneath the snow, whispers call,
Gentle reminders, love's soft thrall.
Amidst the frost, a spark resides,
Hidden joy that warmth provides.

Chill fingers dance on branches bare,
Yet heartbeats echo, vibrant air.
The earth holds secrets, veiled in white,
Awaiting spring's most tender light.

Each fallen flake, a fragile dream,
Shimmers gently, a silken beam.
In winter's grasp, we still believe,
That under layers, we can breathe.

The silence wraps us, soft and deep,
In cozy corners, memories keep.
A flicker glows in dark's embrace,
Promising warmth, a love's trace.

So as we walk on winter's path,
Embrace the chill, forget the wrath.
For every snowflake sings a song,
Of echoes warm where hearts belong.

Lurking Below the Ice-Covered Veil

Beneath the icy, glistening sheet,
Life stirs softly, pulsing discreet.
A heartbeat echoes, muffled, low,
Secrets hidden beneath the snow.

Branches bend with a silent weight,
Nature pauses, holding fate.
Yet, in the depths, a flicker shines,
Awakening dreams in tangled lines.

The stillness speaks of tales untold,
Of whispers soft, of hands to hold.
Buried treasures, waiting for thaw,
Life's resilience, nature's law.

With every chill, the earth gets hushed,
Yet underneath, a warmth is gushed.
The promise lingers, vibrant, bold,
Beneath the ice, life will unfold.

So listen closely to the ground,
For in the frost, a pulse is found.
A dance of hope beneath the freeze,
Waiting for spring's gentle breeze.

Frosted Reverie of the Hidden Wild

In shadows deep, the wild holds breath,
A whispered pause, a dance with death.
Frosted visions cloak the trees,
Silver dreams on winter's breeze.

Each flake that falls, a tale confined,
Of creatures hidden, intertwined.
Soft paw prints fade on whitest ground,
Echoes of life that still abound.

The forest sleeps, yet pulses strong,
Within the stillness, there's a song.
Nature's heart beats, steady, slow,
In frosted reverie, life will grow.

Branches arch like storylines,
Wrapped in white, where light aligns.
In frozen whispers, warmth will rise,
From hidden wilds, beneath the skies.

So let us dream of what will be,
As frost enchants the dormant trees.
For in this hush, we soon will see,
Life's vibrant pulse, wild and free.

Promises of Life in Cold Shadows

In shadows cast by dimming light,
Hope flickers softly, burning bright.
With every breath, the chill draws near,
Yet whispers promise hope right here.

Amongst the frost, our dreams will lie,
Beneath the surface, reaching high.
Each layer deep holds stories spun,
Of life's return when warmth is won.

The quiet murmurs, nature's song,
In icy breath, we still belong.
A tapestry of dreams awaits,
In cold shadows, life radiates.

As winter's grip begins to wane,
And droplets gather, grasping rain.
We stand in faith, with hearts aligned,
For spring's embrace, a love defined.

In every storm, a promise grows,
Within the chill, the warmth still glows.
For life persists, in shadows cold,
A future bright through winter's hold.

Life Waiting for the Thaw

In shadows long and cold they sleep,
Expecting warmth, their secrets keep.
Underneath the ice, life stirs,
A whisper soft, the springtime purrs.

Silent dreams of colors bright,
Seeking sun to end the night.
Yet in this freeze, a promise lies,
Awakening with cerulean skies.

Each flake a kiss from winter's breath,
Holding hearts in quiet death.
Yet hope sleeps not; it waits for light,
To dance again, in pure delight.

The trees stand still, dressed in white,
Each branch a tale, a quiet flight.
Yet beneath this frozen sheet,
The pulse of life will never cease.

When gentle sunbeams start to break,
The world will sing, the ice will shake.
Life waiting still, for warmth's embrace,
In every particle, a tender trace.

Dormant Souls in Chilling Embrace

Under layers, the stillness sighs,
In a world tired of white lies.
Dormant hearts in chilling thrall,
Await the breezes' gentle call.

Beneath the frost, the roots dig deep,
In silence where the shadows creep.
Wrapped in dreams, they bide their time,
In winter's hold, they learn to climb.

Each breath of wind a soft caress,
Carrying whispers of the less.
In frozen arms, the secrets stay,
Until the dawn ignites the day.

The ground will thaw, the aches will cease,
In this pause before release.
Dormant souls, they yearn and wait,
For the sun to open up the gate.

In frozen slumber, life holds fast,
The promise of warmth, an ardent blast.
From chilling grip, they'll rise anew,
In vibrant shades of every hue.

The Silent Chorus of Frosted Fields

Across the fields, a silence reigns,
Crystals glimmer through winter's chains.
Nature sleeps, a soft repose,
In white attire, the earth bestows.

Each flake that falls, a song unfolds,
Of stories whispered, yet untold.
In muted tones, the chorus swells,
Of winter's frost and silent spells.

Branches bare against the sky,
Still, they reach and never die.
A symphony of ice and air,
In stillness found, a beauty rare.

The frost embraces every place,
In its hold, a soft embrace.
Yet deep beneath, the heartbeat thumps,
A melody that softly jumps.

Awaiting spring with hopeful eyes,
This silent choir will rise and rise.
Through winter's breath, a song of grace,
Of life renewed in every space.

Shadows in a White Blanket

Veil of white, a tranquil shroud,
Cloaks the earth, soft and proud.
In shadows cast, familiarity fades,
Beneath the blanket, life cascades.

Each step a whisper on the ground,
The world anew, no idle sound.
Underneath, the secrets weave,
In every fold, they take their leave.

Hushed are voices, gone the rush,
A softening touch, the world is hush.
Time halts within this quiet space,
As dreams are wrapped in winter's grace.

The silence calls, the stillness beckons,
Where warmth awaits and nothing reckons.
In shadows deep beneath the snow,
The heartbeats thrum; they ebb and flow.

As suns will rise, so will they too,
Emerging boldly, bright and new.
In this white blanket, weeds break free,
For beauty blooms in secrecy.

Secrets Buried in Frozen Time

In the stillness, whispers hide,
Memories trapped, like snowflakes glide.
Beneath the frost, stories lie,
Awaiting warmth, a gentle sigh.

The trees, silent sentinels stand,
Guarding secrets of the land.
Echoes of laughter, faint and low,
Yearn for the sun's embracing glow.

Time moves slowly, as shadows dance,
In the cold, we see a chance.
To unearth what's lost in snow,
And let our hidden truths bestow.

With every flake that falls anew,
Buried dreams, waiting to break through.
The frost, a canvas, white and bright,
Holds the echoes of day and night.

Unlock the chest of winter's grace,
With every turn, the past we face.
In frozen time, we seek the light,
To coax the shadows back from night.

The Whispering Heart of Winter

In the hush of falling snow,
Winter's secrets start to flow.
Between the pines, a gentle dream,
The world is wrapped in silver gleam.

Cold winds carry tales untold,
Of ancient nights and hearts of gold.
Each breath a cloud that fades away,
In winter's grip, we long to stay.

The moonlight dances on the ice,
A realm of quiet, soft and nice.
The heartbeats echo, thump and beat,
In winter's arms, we find our heat.

Frosted windows, candle's glow,
Tales of warmth in winters slow.
We gather close, share whispers sweet,
In this cold, our bonds repeat.

Nature's breath, a gentle sigh,
Beneath the stars that drift up high.
In the whispering heart, we find,
The beauty of the chill entwined.

Tucked Away in Icy Cradle

In the quiet, soft and deep,
Nature rests, the world in sleep.
Snowflakes blanket every tree,
A tranquil hush, serenity.

Tucked away in winter's hold,
Stories buried, treasures gold.
Dreaming blooms beneath the frost,
Soon to wake, no vision lost.

Ivy clings to ancient stone,
A tender touch, never alone.
In the cradle, waiting time,
For spring's kiss, a gentle rhyme.

Winter whispers, secrets told,
In every corner, memories fold.
A frozen pond, reflections cast,
Holding moments from the past.

As shadows fade and daylight swells,
In icy dreams, the heart compels.
Awaken now, the warmth will spread,
In nature's cradle, life is fed.

Nature's Sleep in Silvery Shroud

Wrapped in white, the world does rest,
Nature sleeps, its tranquil best.
A silvery shroud, serene and pure,
In winter's arms, we all endure.

Every branch, a crystal dream,
Reflects the sun's soft, golden beam.
Whispers echo through the trees,
A lullaby carried by the breeze.

In the meadows, shadows play,
As night gives life to the next day.
Stars twinkle in a velvet sky,
As all the earth begins to sigh.

In silence, life is gently spun,
Waiting for the warmth of sun.
Underneath the snow, time waits,
For spring's embrace to open gates.

Nature's slumber, deep and wide,
Holds the promise of the tide.
When thawing breath rekindles zest,
From silvery shroud, life is blessed.

The Soft Repose of the Icebound Meadow

The meadow lies in a silent trance,
Blanketed under a diamond glance.
Stillness whispers in the frosted air,
Nature's breath, a gentle, frosty care.

Beneath the ice, life softly sleeps,
While winter's hand its vigil keeps.
Trees stand tall, adorned in white,
Guardians of a world wrapped tight.

Footprints trace where shadows play,
In this calm, where dreams hold sway.
A secret song, the breezes weave,
In the stillness, we believe.

Frosted petals, nature's art,
Capture light, and touch the heart.
Each flake falls, a soft caress,
In cold's embrace, we find our rest.

Revelations from Frost-Kissed Dreams

Awake in slumber, a world of light,
Frost-kissed whispers greet the night.
Dreams unfurl like winter's breath,
In the silence, shadows rest.

Stars glimmer through the icy veil,
As if to tell a soft, sweet tale.
The moon reflects on secrets shared,
Each glint, a moment deeply cared.

Gentle silence holds the night,
In this realm, all feels right.
Wonders spin in frosty streams,
Unraveled here, our truest dreams.

The air is thick with magic's touch,
A breath of hope, we clutch so much.
In every flake, a story's core,
Frost-kissed dreams, we long for more.

Nightfall in the Glittering Snow

As day surrenders to velvet skies,
A blanket of snow in silence lies.
Lamp posts glow like distant stars,
Here in winter, we heal our scars.

Each step crunches, a symphony sweet,
Echoes dance beneath our feet.
Whispers travel on the breeze,
Carrying secrets through the trees.

Snowflakes twirl in a waltz divine,
Nature's canvas, softly aligned.
In twilight's embrace, all seems to blend,
In sparkling stillness, we transcend.

Pine boughs bow with icy grace,
Holding dreams in their frosty embrace.
Nightfall lingers, so serene,
In the glittering world, we glean.

The Gentle Anticipation of Spring

Underneath the winter's shroud,
Hope awakens, soft yet proud.
Snowdrops peek through icy seams,
Whispering of unfurling dreams.

The sun's warm kiss begins to tease,
Breath of life dances in the breeze.
Gentle warmth, a sweet embrace,
As color stirs in nature's grace.

Birds return with songs anew,
Painting skies in shades of blue.
Each note a promise in the air,
Of spring's revival, fresh and rare.

The world transforms as colors blend,
In this cycle, we comprehend.
Life rekindles, hopes take flight,
In the gentle span of light.

Frozen Echoes of Life

In the stillness, shadows play,
Where whispers fade at end of day.
Silent echoes fill the air,
Frozen memories linger there.

Beneath the frost, a heartbeat lies,
Hidden truths as time flies by.
Nature's breath, a quiet song,
In the cold, we all belong.

Trees like giants, bare and bold,
Guard the stories yet untold.
In their silence, secrets hide,
In frozen cores, life will abide.

Snowflakes dance, a fleeting grace,
Softly drifting, finding place.
Whispers of the past remind,
Life's essence in the blind.

As seasons shift, the thaw will come,
With warmth and light, a steady drum.
Yet still within this icy shroud,
Life's echoes sing, soft but proud.

The Winter's Sleeping Heart

In slumber deep, the world does rest,
Cocooned in white, by nature blessed.
The chill holds tight, a gentle squeeze,
While dreams unfold in frosted trees.

Each flake a wish, spun from the night,
Whispered hopes in pale moonlight.
Beneath the snow, a pulse remains,
Awaiting warmth to break the chains.

Silence reigns where rivers froze,
A blanket soft, where nothing grows.
But deep within, a fire waits,
To open wide the winter's gates.

As stars adorn the velvet sky,
The sleeping heart begins to sigh.
Life stirs beneath, a stirring sound,
With promise sweet, the thaw is found.

When spring's first breath begins to tease,
The sleeping heart will wake with ease.
To shed the shroud, to greet the morn,
Of life reborn, where dreams are worn.

Hibernating Whispers

In the quiet, shadows creep,
Nature's secrets, buried deep.
While creatures rest in woven nests,
Whispers linger, as the world rests.

Frosted breath upon the glass,
Time seams slow, as moments pass.
In the cradle of the cold,
Whispers of the brave and bold.

Silk of snow wraps round the ground,
In crisp air, muffled sounds abound.
Life is hushed, a soft embrace,
Within the stillness, there's a grace.

Yet beneath the icy shell,
Lies a story poised to tell.
As days grow long, and warmth returns,
The whispers of life slowly burns.

When spring emerges, bright and clear,
The hibernating dreams draw near.
Awakened by the sun's sweet kiss,
Life resumes, and worlds are bliss.

The Shroud of Frosted Stillness

A shroud of frost drapes o'er the land,
Where silence speaks, and time is manned.
Nature holds her breath in peace,
In this moment, all troubles cease.

Crystals glisten in the dawn,
As daylight breaks, the night is gone.
In delicate lace, the world is spun,
A tranquil canvas, all is one.

Footfalls muffled on the ground,
In this hush, no echo sound.
Each breath of air, a calm delight,
Wrapped in stillness, draped in white.

The trees stand guard with arms outspread,
While dreams weave where the angels tread.
Life awaits, in slumber deep,
Till warmth's embrace begins to seep.

Underneath the calm exterior,
Lies a pulse, strong and superior.
A time will come when earth will stir,
And sunlight's touch brings life to her.

Laid to Rest in Winter's Hold

Beneath a quilt of purest white,
The world lies still in winter's night.
Silent whispers drift and fade,
In nature's love, our hearts are laid.

Icicles hang like crystal tears,
Echoing the dreams of years.
Resting softly, all is cast,
In the cradle of the past.

The trees wear coats of frosty lace,
While shadows dance in graceful space.
Breathless moments, time suspended,
In winter's arms, our sorrows blended.

Stars peek out from skies of gray,
Guarding secrets that softly sway.
The chill, a balm for wounds once bared,
In silence, all our burdens shared.

As dawn arrives with golden hue,
Life stirs anew; the earth is true.
Yet in this hold, we lay at rest,
In winter's grasp, we find our best.

The Silent Repose

In the hush of falling snow,
Whispers tell what hearts may know.
The world sleeps under soft embrace,
In silent fields, we find our place.

Every flake, a tale of old,
Wrapped in warmth against the cold.
Resonates the quiet grace,
Of winter's arms in sweet embrace.

Branches bow with heavy sighs,
Mirroring the muted skies.
Hushed reflections in the night,
Softly glimmering, lost from sight.

Among the drifts, a secret lies,
Beneath the layer, life still thrives.
In peaceful rest, we hear the call,
Of winter's touch, embraced by all.

In stillness found, our spirit glows,
As nature's dance, a sacred pose.
Each moment savored, softly pressed,
In the embrace of silent rest.

Hushed Secrets of the Gelid Ground

Beneath the frost, a tale unfolds,
Where nature's secrets gently hold.
The breath of winter, brisk and clear,
Whispers softly, drawing near.

Shadows linger, stories we weave,
In quiet corners, we believe.
Frozen echoes, tender grace,
In the cradle of this space.

Each layer thick, a waiting dream,
Crystallized in silver beam.
Time suspends its fleeting flight,
In the stillness of the night.

Winter's hush, a sacred trust,
In soft embrace, we bend, we must.
Nature's heartbeat, still and deep,
Within the ground, our secrets keep.

As spring shall come, the thaw arrives,
In warming light, the spirit thrives.
From hushed secrets, life reborn,
In winter's hold, the hope is sworn.

Winter's Secret Garden

In the heart of winter's chill,
A secret garden waits, so still.
Buried treasures rest below,
In whispers soft, the dreams may grow.

Petals folded, colors veiled,
In quietude, the stories sailed.
Underneath the frosty crust,
Life prepares, in nature's trust.

Melodies of silence hum,
In harmony, the seasons come.
Each frozen leaf, a work of art,
Held in time, a gentle heart.

Among the branches, shadows play,
Crafting tales in shades of gray.
Every flake a rare design,
In winter's grasp, our dreams entwine.

As sun creeps in, the thaw appears,
Renewal blooms beyond the years.
In winter's garden, deep and wide,
Life's tender secrets softly bide.

Songs of the Crystallized Earth

In the hush of dawn's embrace,
Emerald stones gleam with grace.
Whispers rise from the deep,
Secrets that the ancients keep.

Mountains sing with a soft breath,
Crystals dance, defying death.
Rivers weave through ages past,
Echoes of a spell that's cast.

Underneath the starry quilt,
Tales of dreams and fears are built.
Nature's heart in every beat,
Froze in time, so pure, so sweet.

Winds carry the voice of stone,
Each note a memory, alone.
In the quiet, truths unfurl,
A rhythm of the crystal world.

Life and rock in gentle dance,
A cosmic bond, a fleeting chance.
Songs of the earth intertwine,
In this realm, all hearts align.

Heartbeats of the Hidden

Beneath the surface, secrets dwell,
In shadows deep, they weave their spell.
Silent whispers call the bold,
Stories of the lost unfold.

Echoes linger where light fades,
In the corners, lost parades.
Softened breaths beneath the stone,
Heartbeats feel forever alone.

Time stands still in the muted night,
Each pulse a soft, forgotten light.
In the depths, a melody sway,
Calling forth the light of day.

Hands grasp at the veils of fate,
In the dark, we hesitate.
Seeking out the paths we knew,
In the longing, we find truth.

Hidden realms and veiled skies,
Whispers weave into our sighs.
Hear the heart that beats within,
A journey lost, where dreams begin.

A Tapestry of Frosted Whispers

In the stillness of the night,
Frosted tales blend dark and light.
Each flake a memory preserved,
A tapestry richly served.

Glimmers dance on icy streams,
Carrying the weight of dreams.
Veils of gold in silver spun,
Whispers of the winter sun.

Painted landscapes wrapped in white,
Secrets hidden out of sight.
Voices thread the chilly air,
In this quiet, hearts lay bare.

Every sigh a breath of lore,
Every step opens a door.
To a world where time stands still,
And dreams are born from winter's chill.

Cascading notes in frosty streams,
Woven softly into dreams.
In the chill, we find our way,
A tapestry of night and day.

The Color of Cold Silence

In the dawn of winter's gaze,
Silence blankets the world's haze.
Colors fade to shades of gray,
In stillness, all words stray.

Frozen breaths in breathless air,
A quiet song, it's everywhere.
Echoes caught in crystal light,
Eyes closed, embracing the night.

Softly whispers drift and glide,
An unseen tide, where dreams abide.
In the shadows, secrets bloom,
The silence sings, the heart finds room.

Through the veil of frosty dust,
In silence, we find our trust.
Every heartbeat paints the void,
A masterpiece, pure and devoid.

As shadows linger, colors swirl,
Fading softly, a quiet whirl.
Here in stillness, we belong,
Caught in the echoes of our song.

Whispers of the Submerged Soil

Beneath the ground, secrets lie,
Roots entangle, reaching high.
The earth's soft breath, a silent song,
Harbors tales where we belong.

Each grain holds whispers of the past,
Stories woven, shadows cast.
In the dark, life's pulse doth fade,
Yet dreams emerge from the glade.

Moonlight dances on soft earth,
Caressing hopes of silent birth.
Nature's rhythm, a calming call,
Nurtures life, enriches all.

As raindrops fall, the soil sighs,
In hidden depths, a world complies.
From stillness grows the wild and free,
The whispers rise, embracing me.

In ancient woods, where stillness reigns,
Life awakens, shedding chains.
Listen closely, the soil speaks,
In its heart, the future peeks.

Ghosts of Summer Under Winter's Watch

In the frost, memories cling tight,
Summer whispers in the night.
Ghosts of laughter, fleeting cheer,
Wander softly, drawing near.

The sun's warm glow now far away,
Yet shadows dance in disarray.
Chilled winds carry tales of yore,
As the hearth's heart beats once more.

Stars shimmer with a distant light,
Echoes of days that felt so bright.
Each flake a story, soft and white,
As winter's mantle holds them tight.

The world sleeps under silvery dreams,
Wrapped in quiet, soft moonbeams.
Even in cold, warmth can be found,
In each whisper, love's profound.

As spring draws near, hearts will thaw,
Bringing life back, a gentle awe.
From winter's grip, hope shall arise,
To chase away the ashen skies.

Frostbound Dreams

Silent are the fields tonight,
Blanketed in purest white.
Frostbound dreams in shadows sleep,
Whispered hopes the silence keeps.

Icicles glisten, sharp and clear,
Reflecting thoughts we hold dear.
The world turned quiet, still as death,
Yet life is stored with every breath.

With every flake that graces ground,
A symphony of peace is found.
In the chill, spirits intertwine,
Nature's beauty, a gift divine.

Stars twinkle like frost-kissed eyes,
Echoes of laughter in the skies.
Though bound in ice, the heartbeats thrum,
Awaiting the warmth that will come.

As the dawn breaks with a soft glow,
Melting dreams begin to flow.
Frostbound, yet not lost in time,
Awaiting the spring's sweet rhyme.

Hidden Hopes in Ice

Beneath the surface, whispers stored,
Frozen secrets, softly poured.
In crystal shells, the dreams are cast,
Awaiting spring to melt the past.

Each breath of winter, cold and clear,
Holds the promise of warmth near.
Encased in ice, bright visions wait,
For the sun to unlock fate.

In twilight hours, shadows glide,
Masked in frost, where hopes abide.
Every glimmer speaks of light,
Hidden treasures, out of sight.

The world, a canvas, painted white,
Yet life stirs under dark of night.
Each frozen leaf, a tale untold,
Of brighter days that will unfold.

When thawing breezes start to play,
Hope emerges, in soft array.
From ice to life, a journey made,
Awakening dreams, unafraid.

Dreams Cloaked in Frost

In the stillness of the dawn,
Whispers weave through silent trees.
Dreams draped in icy lace,
Flicker softly in the breeze.

Footprints ghost the frozen ground,
Memories locked in time's embrace.
Each breath a fleeting sound,
A dance of shadows in this place.

Glistening under morning's glow,
Nature's breath, a soft caress.
Stars retreat, their journeys slow,
As daylight claims the wilderness.

With every heartbeat, hopes take flight,
Frosty tendrils stretching wide.
In this realm where day meets night,
Dreamers find their hearts collide.

Beneath the quilt of white and gray,
Secrets whisper through the trees.
In this world where wishes sway,
Frost-kissed dreams drift on the breeze.

The Subtle Cry of Cold Soil

Beneath the frost, the earth does sigh,
Awakening in shivers deep.
A silent plea, a muted cry,
Where secrets of the springtime sleep.

Each grain a story yet untold,
Held close by winter's gentle hand.
In the darkness, life grows bold,
Beneath a blanket, cold and planned.

The air is thick with tales unheard,
Each breath a bond between the roots.
A language felt, yet never stirred,
In whispers of the hidden shoots.

Frosted silence holds the key,
To dreams that curl within the clay.
Nature grieves but silently,
For warmth that just slips further away.

Soon sun will rise, the thaw will start,
Yet for now, the stillness lingers.
In this hush, we find the heart,
Of life awaiting spring's warm fingers.

Underneath the Powdered Silence

Underneath the powdered snow,
Gentle whispers softly roam.
Each flake a story left to show,
Of places lost but not alone.

In the chill of winter's breath,
The world holds close its dreams at night.
Beneath the depths of frozen death,
A spark of life awaits the light.

Softly sleeping, nature waits,
Wrapped in quiet, soothing grace.
Winter's arms, though rough with fates,
Embrace the stillness, hold the space.

Time flows slow in this serene,
Where shadows drift like falling stars.
In this tapestry so keen,
Nature keeps her hidden scars.

As dawn will break the silence wide,
Beneath the frost, the pulse will rise.
The beauty blooms, the cold will bide,
A symphony beneath the skies.

Cradled by the Winter's Embrace

Beneath the clouds, a blanket white,
The earth rests gently, wrapped in peace.
Winter's chill holds all so tight,
As time and beauty find release.

Each branch, a sculpture, still and high,
Cradled by the frost's soft hand.
Beneath the gray and quiet sky,
Life waits for spring's warm command.

In the hush where shadows play,
The whispering winds weave through the pines.
Crystals dance, then fade away,
In this realm where fate aligns.

Glistening fields, a mirrored glaze,
Capture dreams in cold embrace.
Time pauses, lost in a maze,
Of frozen moments, soft with grace.

Yet in this stillness, hope does cling,
As sunbeams creep through heavy gray.
In time, the earth will wake and sing,
As spring will melt the frost away.

Frost-Kissed Echoes

Silent whispers in the trees,
Frost-kissed echoes float with ease.
Moonlight dances on the ground,
Nature's secrets all around.

Footsteps crunch on frozen grass,
Time stands still as moments pass.
Breath of winter, crisp and bright,
Guides us gently through the night.

Icicles shimmer, casting spells,
A tale of frost that softly dwells.
Stars above, they twinkle clear,
In this world, we hold so dear.

Whirls of snowflakes fill the air,
Painting dreams with utmost care.
Frost-kissed echoes, pure and light,
Whispering softly, taking flight.

Resting Heartbeats of the Cold

Beneath the snow, a heartbeat sleeps,
In winter's arms, the silence keeps.
Frozen rivers, still and deep,
Guarding secrets, quiet, steep.

Branches bare, they reach for gray,
In this stillness, dreams will sway.
Resting heartbeats pulse and hum,
Awaiting spring's sweet tender drum.

Chill of night wraps all in white,
While stars above glow, pure and bright.
Nature breathes a gentle sigh,
As whispered winds begin to fly.

Footfalls soft on glistening ground,
In every shadow, peace is found.
Resting heartbeats of the cold,
A tale of life, forever told.

The Layers of Frost

The layers of frost on window panes,
Draw pictures of nature in soft refrains.
Each crystal forms a timeless tale,
Of chilly nights and winter's veil.

Frosty breath on morning's rise,
Whispers linger beneath gray skies.
In every flake, a dance of light,
Mirrors the magic of the night.

Beneath the surface, life awaits,
As seasons shift and dreams create.
The layers of frost, a fleeting view,
An artful hush, forever new.

With every dawn, the world will change,
While winter paints with strokes so strange.
Layers of frost, a fleeting grace,
A gentle touch in time and space.

Secrets of the Winter's Edge

At winter's edge, where shadows play,
Secrets linger at the close of day.
Softly spoken, truths unfold,
Whispers of warmth in the bitter cold.

Paths of silver, trails of white,
Mark the realms of day and night.
In every flurry, stories blend,
Winter's secrets never end.

Wrapped in blankets, silence thrives,
As the world hushes, stillness dives.
Breath of winter, soft and clear,
Echoes of love, we hold so dear.

Frosty patterns birth delight,
Painting dreams with rays of light.
At winter's edge, we wander free,
Finding solace in harmony.

Secrets Lurking in the Cold

Whispers travel through the breeze,
Frosted tales of bygone days.
Hidden shadows in the trees,
Silent, waiting, in a haze.

Footprints fade with each soft breath,
Ghostly echoes in the night.
Nature's spell, a dance with death,
Concealing secrets from our sight.

Icicles hang like frozen tears,
Memories trapped in crystal clear.
Time stands still as winter nears,
Unraveling tales we hold dear.

Snowflakes fall, a story spun,
Each one unique, a fleeting trace.
Beneath the surface, we have won,
A world alive in quiet space.

Beneath the moon's soft, silver glow,
The cold unveils its hidden lore.
Secrets lurk in shadows low,
A breath away, forevermore.

Beneath the Ice's Tender Caress

A frozen realm of glistening blue,
Where dreams take flight on frigid wings.
Nature's quilt, a gentle view,
Hiding truths the winter brings.

Teardrops form on branches bare,
A lullaby whispers through the snow.
In this stillness, hearts lay bare,
Beneath the ice, where secrets flow.

Caged within a crystal dome,
Life pulsates beneath the shield.
Awaking spirits call this home,
Where each heartbeat is revealed.

A symphony of silence plays,
Frozen notes entwine with fate.
Beneath the ice, in winter's haze,
Lies a world that won't abate.

Echoes of a distant cheer,
Captured in the frosty air.
Beneath the ice, we hold dear,
Tender moments, beyond compare.

Cradled in Winter's Silence

Cradled soft in blankets white,
Winter whispers lull our fears.
Nature's breath, a hush at night,
Embraced in stillness, time adheres.

Muffled sounds of crystal chime,
Waltzing softly on the ground.
In this space, we pause for time,
A sanctuary where peace is found.

Footsteps muffled, spirits rise,
Every flake a sacred gem.
In the frost, hidden sighs,
Life pauses, like a gentle hymn.

Snowflakes twirl in perfect dance,
Each a secret, soft and sweet.
Hold this moment, take a chance,
In silence, our hearts repeat.

Cradled in winter's embrace warm,
The world unfurls in frozen grace.
Safe from chaos, calm from storm,
In quietude, we find our place.

The World Below the Glacial Cover

Beneath the vast and frozen sheet,
Lies a realm where shadows play.
A secret world, both cold and sweet,
Waiting for the light of day.

Icicles form, like daggers hung,
Guardians of the hidden lost.
Songs of silence yet unsung,
Tales of hope amidst the frost.

Echoes dance in crystal halls,
Where memories lie under the weight.
Water flows as nature calls,
Life persists, defying fate.

Tendrils reach through ancient ice,
Touching dreams from ages past.
In quiet depths, all things suffice,
The world waits, tranquil and steadfast.

A glacial cover, a soft embrace,
Holding secrets, year by year.
Unseen wonders, endless grace,
The world below, forever near.

Glimmers of Life in the Frost

In the dawn's soft light, they gleam,
Frost-kissed petals wake from dreams.
Each breath a dance, a stolen sigh,
Glimmers of life, beneath the sky.

Amidst the chill, the spirits rise,
Whispers of warmth, beneath the skies.
Nature's secrets, quietly spun,
In frost's embrace, new journeys begun.

The trees wear coats of icy lace,
Crystals forming, nature's grace.
With each step, the ground will crack,
Glimmers of hope, we won't look back.

An artful quilt, the landscape sleeps,
As silence deep in stillness creeps.
Through winter's grip, life's pulse will beat,
In glimmers bright, our hearts will meet.

And as the snowflakes gently fall,
They write their stories, one and all.
In fleeting moments, we'll behold,
Glimmers of life, in frost so bold.

The Inhabitants of the Icy Abyss

In the depths where shadows play,
Creatures dwell, both night and day.
Silent whispers, tales untold,
In icy waters, brave and bold.

Beneath the waves, the spirits glide,
Among the rocks, they choose to hide.
With shimmering scales, they roam free,
In the abyss, they find their glee.

Frosty currents, secrets weave,
In every tide, they take their leave.
Echoes call, forming a thread,
Inhabiting dreams that seldom tread.

A dance of light, a fleeting glance,
In frozen depths, they'll find their chance.
Within the cold, a warmth will spark,
Together they thrived, in the deep dark.

The mystery thrives, in silence deep,
In the icy abyss, secrets keep.
With every wave, their stories blend,
In this realm, adventure won't end.

Embraced by the Wintry Stillness

In winter's arms, the world abides,
A tranquil hush where cold resides.
Blankets of white, a silent song,
Embraced by stillness, we belong.

Footsteps muffled on the ground,
In a frozen peace, joy is found.
Branches heavy with fleecy grace,
The wintry stillness, a warm embrace.

Time slows down, as shadows stretch,
In nature's quilt, our hearts are etched.
With every breath, a crystal glow,
In this quietude, love will grow.

As daylight fades, the stars appear,
A blanket of dreams, soft and clear.
Embraced by night, we find our rest,
In wintry stillness, we are blessed.

And in the dark, whispers ignite,
Each frozen moment feels so right.
In tranquil visions, hearts will soar,
Embraced by stillness, forevermore.

Twinkling Stars in a White Sea

In a blanket of snow, stars shine bright,
Glimmers of wonder, pure delight.
Each twinkle whispers tales of old,
In a white sea, secrets unfold.

The night sky dances; shadows play,
Twinkling gems guide our way.
Across the vastness, we take flight,
In dreams ignited by soft moonlight.

A canvas stretched, painted in dreams,
Where frosty visions catch the beams.
Each flake a star, unique and rare,
In a wintry sea, magic fills the air.

As echoes rise like gentle tides,
In this embrace, the heart confides.
With every gaze, new worlds align,
Twinkling stars in a white sea, divine.

In the chill of night, we find our spark,
As whispers call from the still dark.
In every moment, our spirits breathe,
Twinkling stars, forever weaves.

Milton Keynes UK
Ingram Content Group UK Ltd.
UKHW010231111224
452348UK00011B/661